Edited by Michael Reidy

Principle
and
Profit

CORPORATE RESPONSIBILITY
IN IRELAND

THE COLUMBA PRESS
DUBLIN 1992

First edition, 1992, published by
THE COLUMBA PRESS
93 The Rise, Mount Merrion, Blackrock, Co Dublin

ISBN 1 85607 053 0

Cover by Bill Bolger
Origination by The Columba Press
Printed in Ireland by
Colour Books Ltd., Dublin

Contents

Introduction

Michael Reidy & Domhnall McCullough

How can profit and principles co-exist in business? What about the responsibilities of employers? What about the responsibilities of employees?

The Dublin Institute of Adult Education was set up in 1951 to examine sociology from a Catholic perspective. In its forty years, it has attempted to look at all developments in sociological thinking from the perspective of Catholic Social Teaching. The papers presented in this book are an attempt to explore, from a number of perspectives, the role of corporate responsibility in today's world. In particular, the focus is on Ireland and the Irish business reality.

Ethics in business have made something of a comeback in recent times in terms of popular discussion and thinking. Not too long ago, the raising of the issue of the ethics of business would not have raised a great stir. All that has changed in the light of the events in Ireland in 1991.

Business cannot be conducted without reference to a code of conduct. Business thrives on competition, but it must take account of realities other than competition. The foundation of all business is the individual person or the people who make up the businesses.

Catholic Social Teaching places the person at the centre of all decision-making, according to Fr John Sweeney in his contribution to this book. His thought-provoking article gives an outline of Catholic Social Teaching on corporate business.

Mark Hely-Hutchinson's contribution focuses on a corporate perspective. He is conscious of the moral responsibility of the business person and proposes the 'newspaper test' as a limiting exercise on business practices.

Peter Cassells, in a union perspective, acknowledges the need for entrepreneurs in today's Ireland if jobs are to be created. He warns against the 'Cute Hoor' syndrome which bedevils Irish business and enterprise culture, and proposes a legally-binding code of behaviour for business people.

Emer Colleran offers an environmental perspective and cites examples, both national and international, of where corporate irresponsibility has resulted in irreparable damage to the environment. Business and government have a responsibility to hand on what they have received in trust to the next generation and not to ravage the environment for national, corporate or personal short-term gain.

Margaret Downes outlines a more socially responsible approach to corporate accounting and annual reports, whereby information on the corporation's effects on the environment and on the local community, and information on customer satisfaction, employee welfare, etc, are separately reported in what might be termed corporate social accounting.

Miriam Hederman O'Brien deals with the role of taxation in

the achievement of social justice and of its potential function as a more equitable distributor of wealth. She stresses the necessity for 'fairness' in taxation, i.e. that persons in the same situation should receive the same treatment.

In his paper on the responsibility of the media, Douglas Gageby engagingly chides us for scapegoating the media as irresponsible, before going on to acknowledge and outline the responsibilities of journalists to their readers and to the truth.

Jack Fitzpatrick sets out the origin of the limited liability concept and its flaws in relation to the just distribution of profits. He points to the importance of profit-sharing in the achievement of social justice and better industrial relations and describes gainsharing as the optimum form of profit-sharing, with its benefits to all parties involved in the well-being of a corporation.

The articles published here were delivered at a seminar organised by the Dublin Institute of Adult Education in association with the Leopardstown Social Study Group which was opened on 1st October 1991 by President Mary Robinson to mark the fortieth anniversary of the Institute's foundation and the centenary of *Rerum Novarum*, which effectively marked the birth of modern Catholic Social Teaching. It is worth recording that planning for the seminar began in October 1990 – long before the various business scandals broke which shocked and outraged the public at the time of the seminar. Pope John Paul II's *Centesimus Annus*, was also published early in the summer of 1991.

The teachings of *Rerum Novarum*, while written over a hundred years ago, still have application today. *Centesimus Annus* underlined that fact. However the teaching cannot be left as just a formal statement of the Church's view but must be given concrete expression by Christians in the corporate and public sectors if equity, ethics and integrity are to prevail in business and if the confidence essential to business transactions is to be re-affirmed. As the Archbishop of Dublin, Desmond Connell, says in his Pastoral Letter for Lent 1992, *Christian Integrity, Does it Matter?*: 'Business can flourish only if there is confidence, and confidence is based on the integrity of members of the business community.' (p.17)

The speakers at this seminar and those who chaired the different sessions, are all people of wide and varying experience in the business world and their views and commitment to standards of ethics in business must make an important contribution to the current debate and thinking in this area.

A Moral Perspective

The Perspective of Catholic Social Teaching

John Sweeney SJ

A case can be made that Ireland's corporate sector should be well briefed about Roman Catholic Social Teaching. A significant number of the same people, after all, look to the one for jobs and a higher standard of living and to the other for help in forming a moral and authentically human perspective on their individual and collective participation in society. The hundredth anniversary of Catholic Social Teaching (1891-1991) was being celebrated in multiple ways within the Christian Churches during 1991, but it probably took the business scandals of the autumn of that year to stir some real interest in a moral perspective on modern business among the men and women gearing up for 1992.

Business people can experience some resistance and fears in themselves to welcoming a Christian voice on corporate business affairs today. They may feel that the Churches are full of advice on how to distribute income but overlook the challenges of generating it. They may fear 'bleeding heart' prescriptions to combat poverty, the practical workings-out of which will only add to the numbers of poor people. They may think of Church people as being used in a wider ideological war against them, as men and women of practical and compassionate make-ups who uncritically adopt radical social and political analyses simply because they were handily available.

Without a doubt, sincere Church members have, on occasion, done each of these things. If we isolate those claiming to speak out of the Roman Catholic social tradition, however, it can be seen that they spoke in error and not as accurate spokespersons for Catholic Social Teaching.

For example, is Catholic Social Teaching so concerned with giving more income to the poor that it overlooks the challenge of generating it? No. Catholic Social Teaching has developed an entirely positive theological and spiritual framework for supporting human *economic endeavour*. It underlines the giveness and gift of creation. It points to the Creator's positive will that the human family, as co-creators with him, through work, ensure that this creation find a principle of harmony and enrichment by its being brought to acknowledge the authority of the human person as an orchestra does its conductor. This makes it possible to speak of helping to generate wealth as a *Christian vocation*.

In fact, despite a steadily clearer analysis that gross super-development in parts of the world is paralysing the human family from taking effective action to tackle evident underdevelopment in much of the rest of it (including regions within industrialised societies), Catholic Social Teaching has resolutely avoided sweeping anti-material goods, anti-technology or anti-growth positions. 'It is not wrong to want to live better,' says *Centesimus Annus* simply (36). And Catholic Social Teaching is aware that, for the majority of people in the world economy at the moment, the path to 'living better' is still through having more. In this sense, therefore, Catholic Social Teaching is aiding and abetting economic activity.

Does Catholic Social Teaching support initially plausible but ultimately disastrous policies for redistributing income? The main concern of business people here would be that religious sanction can be too easily given to policies that interfere with the *free market* and, ultimately, wreak havoc with people's lives. That's not true. Since its reputed birth in 1891, Catholic Social Teaching has condemned every absolutisation of the free market which was sanctioning exploitation or indifference to economic distress. However, today it is clear in its praise of the free market ('the most efficient instrument for utilising resources and effectively responding to needs,' *CA* 34, 'offering secure advantages,' *CA* 40, etc.). It has also grown in clarity that reliance on the free market requires a strong surrounding culture which is capable of maintaining in people a strong awareness that having money and spending it is a means to living and not its purpose, and a firm legal and institutional framework to harness the play of free markets to the ends that society has chosen for itself.

Not only this, but Catholic Social Teaching is indebted to its struggle with the former communist versions of socialism in Central and Eastern Europe for a clear articulation of the value and importance 'for the individual and for the common good' (*The Social Concern of the Church*, 1987, n 15) of *economic initiative,* or the freedom for people in the economic sphere to deploy their resources as they see best. It has also come to acknowledge entrepreneurship, 'the ability to foresee both the needs of others and the combinations of productive factors most adapted to satisfy those needs' (*CA* 32), as a *source* of wealth today, with all that that implies for remuneration. Finally, Catholic Social Teaching talks with considerable admiration of the existence and functioning of very large corporations which it is possible to view as 'chains of solidarity' (*CA* 43), 'extensive working communities' where 'diligence, industriousness, prudence in undertaking reasonable risks, reliability and fidelity in interpersonal relationships, courage in carrying out decisions which are difficult and painful but necessary' are virtues which are fostered (*CA* 32). This is not the language of a tradition which is oblivious to the complexity of the modern business economy.

A third difficulty that business people can have with Church pronouncements on corporate affairs is the belief that they tend frequently to be ideologically biassed. (Sometimes, it is possible to read a complaint here that the ideological bias is merely in the wrong direction.) The Church's sole standpoint for commenting on what appear complex and secular economic affairs is its understanding of the human person and, therefore, of the requirements and pitfalls of human society.

'(The Church's) action in earthly matters such as human advancement, development, justice, the rights of the individual, is always intended to be at the service of humanity, and of the human person as she sees that person in the Christian vision of anthropology that she adopts. She does not need to have recourse to ideological systems in order to love, defend and collaborate in the liberation of the human person: at the centre of the message of which she is the depositary and herald she finds inspiration for acting in favour of solidarity, justice and peace, and against ... whatever attacks life.'
(Pope John Paul II, *Puebla Address*, III.2)

The bias of Catholic Social Teaching is people and an awareness of their grandeur and their weakness. This makes
Catholic Social Teaching sensitive and receptive to the view
of the economy from the working person's shoes, giving it a
labour rather than an ideological bias. The Church and
labour movements, after all, are close to and helping organ-
ise the same people. Catholic Social Teaching is now hope-
ful that the closing of the cul-de-sac of marxist socialism to
the labour movement will see this common ground being
built on. That fact is that, because of the long flirtation
labour movements have had with marxism, the interest to
build together scarcely existed. Catholic Social Teaching
now sees the way ahead in pragmatic rather than ideological terms:

'The Church has no models to present; models that are
real and truly effective can only arise within the framework of different historical situations, through the efforts
of all those who responsibly confront concrete problems
in all their social, economic, political and cultural aspects
... ' (CA 43).

Catholic Social Teaching does not take economic growth for
granted. It is not contemptuous of free markets and believ-
ing it knows better ways. It is not a stalking horse for an ideo-
logy hostile to business. These observations, however, only
point to the challenge of articulating just what the perspective of Catholic Social Teaching on corporate business *is*.

A Civilisation of Work
Catholic Social Teaching emphasises that economic activity
takes place in the context of a wider culture, a culture which
must support it and direct it. Why do we want to earn

more? Why do we want to consume more? When our multiple investment accounts are thriving and our third home is fully equipped, then what?

'Economic freedom is only one element of human freedom. When it becomes autonomous, when the human person is seen more as a producer or consumer of goods than a subject who produces and consumes in order to live, then economic freedom loses its necessary relationship to the human person and ends up by alienating and oppressing the person.' (*CA* 39)

It might seem that today our culture is centrally about the pursuit of a better standard of living, that some notion of the 'good life' is what keeps us all co-operating minimally with each other. Catholic Social Teaching challenges us to articulate what precisely we mean by an acceptable 'standard of *living*' and 'the *good* life'. If it is primarily the level of consumption we can enjoy without regard for how people participate in the generation of it, it warns us that we will end up with a society where consumer goods and services have multiplied but where the quality of life and, in particular, our solidarity with each other are abysmal. A section of society will enjoy ever more extensive possessions while another section will experience failure and debate their options of resignation, envy or hate. We can see this developing in Ireland today: on the one hand, the advent of super-luxury facilities for the rich who gain prestige by flaunting their ability to indulge extravagant whims and, on the other hand, the deepening unemployment of local authority housing estates where people indulge their dreams by buying lotto tickets (the world skillfully evoked by Alan Parker's film, *The Commitments*).

What has gone wrong? We saw that Catholic Social Teaching takes no issue with wanting to live better. It argues, however, that living better for a human being *includes working better* and cannot be attained at the cost of ceasing to work or working in a way that is less respectful of one's dignity. An acceptable standard of living must include working (just as it does, for example, adequate nutrition). Catholic Social Teaching moves work from being a means 'normal' people use to acquire the standard of living they want, to being a constituent part of it.

In other terms, the Church points out that purchasing power alone, no matter how great, cannot bring anyone a decent standard of living or quality of life. A life worthy of the human person features work.

'Through work a person not only transforms nature ... but she or he also achieves fulfilment as a human being ... in a sense becomes more of a human being ... A person must work ... because her or his own humanity requires work in order to be maintained and developed. Work corresponds to a person's dignity, expresses this dignity and increases it. Even when it is accompanied by toil and effort, work is still something good.'
(*On Human Work*, 1981, nn 9, 16.)

Casual experience of life in Ireland today is sufficient to confirm this insight. Certainly, those who are familiar with the lives of unemployed people know that even tripling the payments they receive in unemployment compensation would not solve the root problem. Stress associated with financial worries could be expected to lessen, but not that associated with boredom, a sense of rejection by society and, generally, a future-less and feature-less life. At the upper end of the income scale, evidence also abounds that even quite ostentatious levels of consumption – in the context of a life bereft of work – does nothing to guarantee happy and healthy individuals, families or communities.

Catholic Social Teaching is aware that 'all human activity takes place within a culture and interacts with culture' (*CA* 51), and has taken a strong stand in favour of viewing the human person as 'homo laborens' first and 'homo consumens' only second. It sees a powerful cultural current today leading people to exalt their roles and entitlements as consumers and to find and place their self-identity and self-fulfilment primarily through the standard of living they can command, through 'having'. It takes odds with this culture or, rather, regards it as the capitulation of culture to economics.

> 'The culture which our age awaits will be marked by the full recognition of the dignity of human work ... Because the relationship between the human person and work is radical and vital, the forms and models according to which this relationship is regulated will exercise a positive influence for the solution of a whole series of social and political problems facing each people. ... Thus the solution to most of the serious problems related to poverty is to be found in the promotion of a true civilisation of work. In a sense, work is the key to the whole social question. ... Just work relationships will be a necessary precondition (also) for a system of political community capable of favouring the integral development of every individual.' (*Instruction on Christian Freedom and Liberation*, 1986, nn 82-83)

All the stakeholders in a business (employees, managers, investors, customers) must accept that the better standard of living which everyone is pursuing, in fact requires work as a constitutive part of it. This does not involve harnessing business in a crude way to the goal of job creation. No doubt many industries in Ireland today could become much more labour-intensive if technology were shelved and wages cut by two-thirds. However, the logic of being committed to work as an integral element of human well-being means that Catholic Social Teaching also supports technology (an 'ally of human work' when it reduces wear and tear damaging to the human person) and the payment of decent wages ('A just wage is the concrete means of verifying the justice of the whole socio-economic system.' *On Human Work*, n 19).

However, the central importance attached to work in human life by Catholic Social Teaching means that what passes today as successful *financial* performance on the part of a company is not enough. It may be that dividends are being boosted to shareholders, salaries and wages raised for employees, and prices being reduced to customers. Each of these measures, however, only addresses people's purchasing power (considers people only as consumers). If these financial benefits to shareholders, staff and customers have been purchased at the price of working a smaller labour force less humanely (making some workers unemployed and extracting shift-work or systematic overtime from those remaining, not to mention six and a half day working from senior management), this company, argues Catholic Social Teaching, is failing in its principal moral obligations to society.

Catholic Social Teaching is not seeking to place good financial performance in opposition to the expansion and improvement of jobs. It is a prevailing economic theory and

19

practice which has done that. While companies rightly seek profit (*CA* 34), Catholic Social Teaching regards profit not primarily as yet-to-be-distributed dividends, wage and salary increases, and price cuts, but as potential new salary and wage packets in a society hungry for work. The immediate stakeholders in a corporate business must acknowledge that, in addition to their traditional roles, they are stewards for a group of economic and human assets that are part of a wider community's economic and social potential.

'The purpose of a business firm is not simply to make profit, but is to be found in its very existence as a *community of persons* who in various ways are endeavouring to satisfy their basic needs, and who form a particular group at the service of the whole of society.' (*CA* 35)

This vision of the human person needs to be addressed seriously by every business corporation in Ireland today. It is an unconvincing side-step to say, 'We are not in the business of jobs.' Of course no corporation can say that its business is jobs and no more, but nor should it say its goal is profits and no more. Corporate business takes place within a wider culture and society. Our culture and our society are giving the clear message that Irish people want not merely to consume but to be accorded the dignity of consuming *as workers*. We consume in order to live. But living fully is impossible without that activity constitutive of human living which we call work.

A quality work experience, and the expansion of the number of people participating in that collective experience, is, in fact, the bottom line of what Irish society and culture today is asking of corporate businesses. Profits, penetration

of export markets, technological innovation, design exper-
tise, quality products or services, a harmonious relationship
with the environment, good links with local communities,
are so many means to this end. Clear espousal and commitment to this end on the part of corporate business is, it
seems to me, a precondition of widespread social support
and enthusiasm for the many efforts that will be needed to
build stronger export companies in Ireland today.

Corporate business in Ireland today, no matter what its
nature, is hitched, for good or ill, to whatever our performance will be in the new Single Market. Let us turn to that.

A Historical Role for Corporate Business Today
If it is *appropriate* that a moral discourse about the role of
corporate business in Ireland be developed in company
boardrooms and organisations like the IMI, CII and the FIE,
(and not just in theological faculties and by Church people),
the advent of the Single European Market and the prospect
of Economic and Monetary Union within the European
Community is making it *necessary*. This is because the
Single Market, and the constraints on independent national
initiatives that are part and parcel of EC membership, are
giving the role of corporate enterprise a whole new power
for good or ill in our country today. Why is this?

Irish society wants more jobs to be available on the island of
Ireland today. Otherwise, we will continue further down
the road to becoming a dependent region without the
degree of internal strength characteristic of a national economy. A permanent outflow of people of working age will
have, as its counterpart, return flows of tourists, pensioners
and family members back on visits. But where are jobs to
come from?

We are sadder and wiser today and know where sustainable jobs on the scale required cannot come from. They did not come from our turning our back on the world economy and building one of Europe's most protected economies (the industrial drive based on import-substitution begun in 1932). They did not come, on the scale required, from the wholesale arrival of multinational companies and an unprecedented flood of their sophisticated exports leaving our shores (the IDA-led industrial policies that began in the 1960s). They did not come from fiscal expansion and public borrowing (the Irish response to the huge shift in the terms of trade brought about by OPEC's oil-price rises). Unless we take the defeatist attitude that our present employment creation is really all that can be reasonably demanded of us, we are left with only one option: that everyone do their part to help bring about more indigenous firms that are capable of providing goods or services of a quality that Europe and the world wants.

The debate on the most appropriate industrial policy for Ireland continues unabated. There is considerable consensus that what we most need are more large exporting companies with deep roots in the Irish economy. This means companies larger in scale than tends to be the case with Irish-owned companies at present, but with stronger linkages to the rest of the economy than characterise our present multinational subsidiaries. Only the development of such companies can get us away from the present ludicrous position where, for example, an output growth in manufacturing of some 24 per cent over a five year period (1980-84) was associated with a 2.2 per cent growth in GNP. (Finland had an 11 per cent manufacturing growth helping it to a 10.7 per cent growth in GNP over the same period!)

The prominent position of agriculture in our national economy is no compensation for this weakness in our manufacturing sector either. We have been so unsuccessful in developing linkages between our farms and our industry that currently only 3 per cent is added to the value of our agricultural raw materials by industry, whereas the European average is 15 per cent. So while our European partners brace themselves for labour shortages and fresh waves of immigrant labour in the 1990s, here we are alone bleating that our young population (which the rest of Europe envies) or technology (of which the rest of Europe has much more) is the cause of our unemployment.

Readers are reminded of these facts only in order to underline how *one type* of corporate business activity is widely recognised as having a quite historic role to play on this island at present. The defining characteristic is not the nature of ownership. Private sector, semi-State or multinational is not the issue. (Gilbeys Ireland, which has produced one of the country's most successful export innovations in the last twenty years, with a very high degree of domestic value-added, is owned by Grand Metropolitan, a UK-based multinational. Aer Lingus, which is State owned, has developed a hugely successful business in overhauling and servicing the fleets of other airlines.) The key characteristic is that the business activity in question generate as much demand as possible for the skills of our people and other outputs of the Irish economy, and that it market a quality good or service for which there is a real demand.

This type of corporation, and the people who can create them, are being asked to shoulder a quite historic task today by Irish society. Why 'historic'? Because the steadily deepening stakes of membership of the European Community – viewed from one angle – have been taking out of the hands of Irish policy-makers successive instruments that used to be available at the macro-economic level to stimulate job creation. (Entry in 1973 initially involved giving up the right to set tariffs and quotas independently; entering the European Monetary System in 1979 involved surrendering the right to independent devaluations of the Irish pound; signing the Single European Act in 1987 committed us to hand over for even more intense scrutiny our whole battery of incentives for industry to see if, in any way, they distort competition; negotiating Economic and Monetary Union will see, minimally, close co-ordination of national budgets so less autonomy for Irish Ministers of Finance and, maximally, a single currency and monetary policy and virtually nil autonomy for the Irish Central Bank.)

Will this gradual surrender of macro-economic policy instruments and the acceptance that we are, in fact, one part of a larger economy, lead to more jobs in Ireland? The answer will depend more than ever on the quality of the *micro-economic* decisions that are made at board and company level. In a real way, the more the European script has directed that our government ministers and senior officials in agencies like the Central Bank and the IDA move from centre-stage, the more it is inviting entrepreneurs and industrialists committed to our society's number one agenda to move forward and take the limelight.

Let us take the significance of the Structural Funds. To some extent, their being doubled in size was the sweetener to convince this country to sign the Single European Act. The Irish Government had argued the case that the advent of the Single Market would place companies based in Ireland at a huge competitive disadvantage if no more were done. Considerably increased investment in roads, ports, human resources and the like were needed to ensure a level playing field. This argument was accepted, at least in part (I will not go into the question here of the adequacy of the Structural Funds to the regional challenge in Europe, or of whether the Community's commitment to 'economic convergence' is more nominal than real). My point is that all the increased expenditure that is taking place at present thanks to the doubling of the Structural Funds will not, of itself, generate fresh exports and on-going jobs. Unless there are company boards, company managements and company workforces in Ireland hungry to get more and better goods and services out, the better port facilities, roads etc., are as likely to swell the volume of goods and services coming in! Where are the companies bursting to have more rapid transport networks with the Continent and better trained workers? Which are the corporations based in Ireland likely to capture a bigger share of the European market thanks to much lower transport costs and much improved linguistic skills on the part of their employees?

Truly, business corporations in Ireland today have moved centre stage. If they do not respond, if enterprise or economic initiative in Ireland is associated primarily with playing the property or stock markets, if lobbying Kildare Street or Fitzwilton House for incentives and grants is replaced by lobbying Brussels, if technology is greeted by management as a means to tighter control of a smaller workforce (and by unions as means to higher wages for those selected out to work with it), then this economy and this country can settle down to being a somewhat charming, acceptably underdeveloped region within Europe.

Unless corporate business in Ireland not merely survives but expands within the Single European Market, it will be hard to see Ireland retaining a presence in a considerably enlarged Community (of 16, 20, 24 member States?) anything akin to that which we now have. As things stand we are less than one per cent of the Community's population, and a smaller percentage of Europe's GNP. In a bigger Community, sheer logic may mean we eventually find our proper place on a Council of European Regions, swapping notes with Galicia and Sicily, rather than in whatever structure will succeed to the present Council of Ministers.

For Ireland to remain a significant member of the European Community, more jobs must become available on this island rather than in Munich, Milan or Frankfurt. For this to happen, the key role in the 1990s will be played by business corporations. This is not tantamount to writing the Irish Government out of the script. A solidly-based analysis identifies major obstacles to the emergence within a late-industrialising country like Ireland of large, indigenous exporting companies. This analysis assigns a key role to government in helping indigenous companies to surmount those obstacles. Traditional instruments of fiscal and monetary policy may be losing their significance but government can, and must, assist the development of dynamic State and private sector companies.

Practical Issues for Corporate Ethics
Will corporate business in Ireland today assume its historic role? Is society wise to think, even for a moment, that what is good for Ireland PLC is good for us all? Given the quite disappointing performance of the Irish private sector in this country since Independence, would anyone in their right senses now give it a leading role?

Two conclusions emerge from this article that bear on these questions. First, it is only corporate business of a very particular sort which is deserving of broad national support. Secondly, there is no alternative. In this last section, a third conclusion will be drawn and developed. It is that this critical dependence of our society on corporate business today vitally requires that the moral character to match it be forthcoming.

The Implications of Smallness

This last observation can be developed by drawing on recent events. Ireland is a small society and a small economy. This can be a blessing or a curse. It is a blessing when the rapid and frequent communication that is possible, when the sense of being in it together against overwhelming odds, when a truly common culture and a shared economic analysis, all give our corporations, government departments, state agencies, research bodies and trade unions the means to implement co-ordinated and flexible strategies and responses. However, this smallness is a curse when the inevitable extent to which the same people keep meeting, and needing, each other in different roles opens opportunities for individual gain capable of dissolving the moral character of key people. I am quite aware that to argue for consensus and co-operation across the board in fostering some large exporting companies with deep roots in the Irish economy implies more, rather than less, links between boards, agencies, politicians, consultants, and the like. The extraordinary abuse to which this strategy is open (as when the same consultants who help design a Government policy benefit enormously from the subsequent implementation of it, or when personal and political considerations intervene to make a state agency or public officials less rigorous than

27

they would otherwise have been in their relationships with a particular company, or when the senior staff of a company being prepared for privatisation make large personal fortunes out of the subsequent implementation of the privatisation plan, or when 'favours' are traded between individuals in high office – alas, examples are not hard to come by at the moment), however, does not make the strategy the wrong one.

Worker Participation

One way to help limit the opportunity for abuse arising from the smallness of our economy is to give much greater national priority, than we are hitherto, to the development of greater participation by employees in their own companies. The question of worker participation, with all the attendant matters of company disclosure and the prerogatives of management, is, perhaps, one of the hottest issues to have come up for discussion at European Community level. The intense lobbying of multinational enterprise which succeeded in blocking the 'Vredeling' directive of 1983 (by which the 'dominant' company in a group of companies – the New York or Tokyo head office! – would have had to provide the information for subsidiaries to be able to inform and consult with employees *before* taking a major decision affecting them) and the disdain in Britain for the European Social Charter (its articles 17 and 18 encourage 'information, consultation and participation for workers') should not blind us, in this country, to the need for, and great advantage of, a much greater formal role for employees in the life of their company.

It is surely the case that, if Irish society is to solidly support the fostering of a limited number of large, indigenous enterprises, then these enterprises will have to be seen to be welcoming and fostering the responsible participation of their workforces. Just as the health of our economy today is dictated by the health of the firms which make it up, so too the level of participation and responsibility in our civic and social life is affected by how people experience their subjectivity in their place of work. If a person feels treated like a moron or a potential problem all the time at work, she or he is unlikely to be a model of initiative or responsibility in activities that take place at evenings or on week-ends.

Of course, Catholic Social Teaching is solidly in support of finding new legal and organisational structures that would better reflect the real complementarity of labour and capital.

'Recognition of the proper position of labour and the worker in the production process *demands* (emphasis added) various adaptations in the sphere of the right to ownership of the means of production.'
(*On Human Work*, n 14)

'(Catholic Social Teaching) recognises the legitimacy of workers' efforts to obtain full respect for their dignity and to gain broader areas of participation in the life of industrial enterprises so that, while cooperating with others and under direction of others, they can "work for themselves" through the exercise of their intelligence and freedom.' (*CA* 43)

The underlying concept here is that work is only truly *human* work when it is not coerced or manipulated but is the free act of a person whose intelligence and physical capabilities are being voluntarily engaged in a task with others.

Maximum Remuneration

A final reflection on what the development of moral character in corporate business today implies is this: It should be unacceptable to anyone that ownership or management of a profitable enterprise (whose very profitability is partly due to an improved infrastructure and a better trained workforce paid for from public and EC funds, and so on) should be used as a lever to secure personal financial rewards on a mega scale. It is fair to describe Irish society today as engaged in a vast collective endeavour to restructure and expand the national economy so as to allow more Irish people to find satisfying work at home. For some, this has involved unemployment, emigration and temporary work contracts. That it has involved six-figure salaries and the amassing of personal fortunes for others is a cultural abdication to economics and a total rupture of solidarity. Catholic Social Teaching has never supported 'egalitarianism'. It lends no support to measures for 'levelling down incomes'. It does, however, insist that a proportion in the way income is distributed in society be always guarded. It underlines that 'the basis for determining the value of human work is not primarily the kind of work being done but the fact that the one who is doing it is a person.' (*On Human Work*, n 6) If this is so, how can some boards *morally* defend the approval of remuneration packages to key staff that makes those staff into beings from another planet by comparison to what staff employed in cleaning and such humbler tasks are being paid? In the decisions of company boards, there should be sensitivity in settling remuneration for top executives to the moral character of the company as 'a society of persons'

(*CA*, 43) and to the ineradicable links between that company and the wider society in which it operates, where hard decisions are constantly being made as to what can be "afforded' in looking after its poorest and most vulnerable members. In a given society at any time, people of moral character will know – without the need for any legislation – that there is a level of income above which no one, no matter what his or her function or achievements, should be paid.

One positive side effect that I see in the sorry situations of recent months surrounding the Goodman group, Greencore, Telecom Éireann and NCB is the penetrating light that has been thrown, for all too brief a moment, on the business interests and personal lifestyles of a minority in Irish business. People who are poor and unemployed are, by comparison, used to being the subject matter of investigations and research. This author, personally, learned more about the forces that shape the Irish economy today, and about how wealth is generated, in reading the details of these business scandals than from reading any NESC or ERSI report. It may be timely that these scandals broke in the run up to 1st January 1993. The moral character of corporate business in Ireland is not an esoteric issue. It is vital to our prospects as a people.

A Corporate Perspective

Mark Hely Hutchinson

I have been asked to start by considering some of the issues which face businessmen of integrity when operating in the tough business world of today. I stress that I shall look at it, not from the perspective of a TV businessman like J.R. Ewing, but from the view of a thinking Irishman who happens to be in business.

May I start by making a point which will be obvious to the business reader, but perhaps not so obvious to everyone else. That point is that the commercial success and survival of the enterprise is fundamental to any business decision. There is no point in having a commercial enterprise which is so committed to doing the 'right thing' that it runs itself into the ground in commercial terms; if it does this, it will no longer provide employment to its staff or income to its owners.

You may think this point is a bit far-fetched. But there was the case, come years ago, of an Australian company which gave excellent pension rights to its employees and also guaranteed the future contributions. When the company got into difficult trading conditions, the Pension Trustees called the guarantee and effectively put the company into liquidation. So achievement of long-term commercial success is an objective which must always be kept in the forefront.

But let me put this point about the commercial imperative into balance. I strongly believe also that the pursuit of profitability and commercial success must be governed by a moral code which ensures that the firm conducts its affairs with integrity and with concern for the welfare of the community in which it operates. I do not think that these two requirements are in conflict for most of the time. But there are circumstances where they seem to be in conflict. And these conflicts are what I want to talk about in this paper..

I would therefore like to divide my paper into three sections. The first is about the role of management in setting the standards of the corporation. In the second, I shall describe some areas where conflicts do arise. The third part will be about the standards of personal responsibility of managers within corporations. I will end with some conclusions which you may like to debate.

1. The Role of Management

Business Schools and other places of education will offer you as many definitions of the process of management as you can find books. Most of them suggest that the principal role of management is to 'allocate resources' to optimise the performance of the firm. I would take issue with the simplicity of this approach. I believe strongly that the primary task of management is to 'set the tone' in the widest possible sense.

Management is responsible for setting the direction of the firm, for setting the criteria by which top management will evaluate the performance of its units and of its people, and finally for setting the style of the firm in relation to its customers, its suppliers, its staff and its community. Some of you may argue that what I have described is the role of the Board – and you are right. But the translation of all this to the organisation is the primary function of management.

It follows from this definition of the role of management that there is a risk that one of the elements will get overlooked. For example, if the firm is pursuing very actively a new market direction and has put in place strong incentives to ensure that people in the firm meet demanding criteria for personal reward, there will be danger that the third element (i.e. the style of the firm) will be ignored. This situation, I suspect, conforms to the outsider's perspective of the 'typical' hard-nosed business approach. It is not, however, my experience.

As many of you will know, management uses a number of devices to achieve this process of 'setting the tone'. Typically, the firm would have a 'Mission Statement' which sets out its market and profit objectives, but also sets out some of the style elements as well. Mission statements normally include a commitment to integrity (towards the customer, staff, etc), to responsibility to the community and so on. However, I would have to be the first to admit that making a formal statement is one thing; the real process of communicating intangible things like style takes place by the example of top management. So a firm which has a stated commitment to integrity is unlikely to persuade its staff to behave in this way if key members of top management are seen to be behaving in a totally different manner in their own affairs. This is the crux. And this is the reason why I shall address in a few minutes the personal ethics of managers and others. But first I want to talk about some areas of conflict.

2. Some Areas of Conflict

The conflicts arise because a normal business has a number of 'stakeholders'. The most important ones are the owners (shareholders), the employees, the customers and the community. Obviously you can elaborate this model to include a number of other interested parties. There are some areas of potential conflict which differ according to the corporate structure. For example, the mutual structure was evolved to prevent conflicts between customers and owners by making the customers or suppliers also the owners. I shall address myself to the problems that arise in a normal publicly quoted company.

Corporate Donations

There is one area of conflict between stakeholders which is often brought up. This is the whole area of 'corporate donations'. Here the conflict issue is simple. It is the owners' money that you are giving away. Is that in the owners' interest? The reality is that large firms do not operate in a vacuum. They operate within (and depend heavily upon the goodwill of) a community from whom their workforce is drawn and from whom many of their customers also come.

This notion is much more obvious to a company which has consumer customers – as in the case of both the major companies for whom I worked. Indeed, for a company like either of these, there are day-to-day contacts with the representatives of the community in one way or another. The logic of participating in activities which benefit the community is more or less inescapable. So, my conclusion in this area is that participating in activities which benefit the community is inherently in the company's (and therefore the shareholders') interest, even where direct commercial benefit does not flow from the action taken. Corporate top management should not really need much convincing about this – and indeed it is my experience that they do not.

Redundancy

Let me give a couple of other types of examples, where the issues are a bit more difficult. Suppose the company is in financial difficulties because its market has declined and the costs are now too high. From the owners' point of view the obvious thing is to cut costs; this will mean laying off staff. Is this the right thing to do? It is hardly in the interest of the staff – or is it?

I have been involved in staff and other major cost reductions on a number of occasions and quite frankly I do not think that there is a real conflict. The reality is that if you do not cut the costs, the company is going to fail and then no member of the staff will have a secure job. Is it not better that you lay off a minority for the protection of the majority? The issue is one of survival. I will grant you that I have been lucky in this area. Both the major companies that I have worked for have been well enough managed to be able to afford a gradual staff reduction programme which was carried out in the most caring way practical – for example no forced redundancies, enhanced terms for voluntary early retirement and so on. Under those circumstances, the goodwill of many of the people laid off was retained and they exist today as reasonably contented pensioners of a much stronger company.

I am aware of the limitation of my own experience. In takeover situations, particularly contested takeovers where the final price paid is higher that the economic price, the guidelines I have been advocating seldom seem to apply, though I do not have personal experience of such situations. Acquiring companies ignore such 'caring' guidelines when 'slimming down' the acquired company to earn a good return on the inflated acquisition price. There is a real dilemma here. Human principles suggest that you should care equally for the staff of the acquired company as you would your own. In reality, the acquired company may need very drastic cuts to make it viable. There are no simple solutions.

Tax Avoidance

Another example. It is obviously in the interest of all stakeholders that the company remains financially strong. This will include minimising the tax bill, to maximise the after-tax profits. Some issues inevitably arise about the techniques for doing this. Some techniques are 'at the edge' of the law – you may get away with them, or you may not. Where is the dividing line for a businessman of integrity?

Again my experience has not been completely typical. Both the major companies I worked for had reason, because of the business they were in, to maintain good relations with the Revenue Commissioners and were therefore unwilling to push the limits of the law; other companies would not be so shy about testing the limits. In practice I believe that there is a simple test for most questions in this area: if you would not be happy to see what you are proposing reported in the business columns of a reputable newspaper, then you shouldn't do it. That test has obviously been ignored in some recent cases in this country.

Executive Remuneration

An issue which is closely related to the previous one is the question of remuneration of executives. (This issue is particularly acute for state-owned commercial companies whose executive remuneration is constrained by civil service rules.) Clearly it is right, in the interest of the company and its stakeholders, that you get the best available executives; and they must be adequately paid.

How far should you go in finding tax-avoidance devices for your executives? Everyone will have different answers to this question, but I suggest that the same 'newspaper test' applies. If you would be unhappy to see your remuneration arrangements reported publicly, then I think you have probably gone too far. This certainly applies to quoted companies and I suggest that it should be equally relevant to state-owned companies.

3. Standards of Personal Ethics in Business

Let me now go on to my third topic – that of standards of personal ethics in business. Three decades ago, business ethics were not really an issue. Today, if one is to believe the politicians and the media, standards seem to be slipping fast. Some of this is media hype, but some of it is reality. There is a cynical definition of 'a dacent man' as someone 'who would not do you down unless he had to'. It's all too easy for such a joke to become accepted practice – but I fear for our society if it does so.

Reflecting, some time back, on the highly publicised trial of Ernest Saunders and his fellows, I often wondered if such major breaches of the law and of normal honest practice could happen here. I thought that in Ireland we were unlikely to see such things, if only because the personal rewards here are so much smaller. But recent events make me wonder.

It is also a worrying thought that if some of the practices which took place in London and New York were to happen here, our legislation is almost certainly not adequate to bring the culprits to justice. There have already been a couple of cases which demonstrate this weakness. I believe we should all worry about that.

I do not want to be drawn into commenting in detail on events which have featured in our own business community in the past year or so. Indeed some of them are effectively *sub judice*. I am referring, of course, to the cases of major companies which have got into trouble because they took actions which failed my 'newspaper test' or because they made statements which turned out not to be true. You can all identify these cases for yourselves.

What does concern me is the conflict of personal interest involved; and in particular, the implication, in a number of these cases, that senior executives in major companies do not understand their 'trustee' relationship to the company for which they work; they seem not to understand that there can be a 'conflict of interest' between their personal benefit and the benefit of the company – or worse still, some appear to think that the company only *exists* for their personal benefit. And some boards of Directors, perhaps unwittingly, are seen to be accomplices to this view.

A defence is sometimes made that the executive concerned is a large shareholder. It is all too easy for an executive who owns a significant share of a company – especially if it is a controlling share – to ignore the interests of the other shareholders; we can see examples of this all too frequently.

In law, and in good practice, there is no difference between executives who have no stake in the firm that they work for and those who have a significant stake; in each case (unless the executive owns 100% of the firm) there is a real difference between the benefit of the company and that of the executive. To stay within the law and within any reasonable ethical code, this distinction must be scrupulously observed. I do not believe that senior executives cannot understand these points. I am forced to conclude that a few conveniently lose sight of them. What is it that causes intelligent people to lose sight of obvious facts? One can ask the same questions, too, about insider trading – but here, quite frankly, under the new Companies Act, it is arguably illegal for a director *ever* to trade in his or her company's shares. That is asking for the law to be broken.

There is an undeniable connection between personal moral standards in a community and the consequent business standards. These slippages, that I have been talking about, are largely the product of the economic environment of the last two decades. Very high levels of personal taxation and a tax system which has been characterised by opportunities for evasion has led to the widely held view that it is reasonable to cheat the tax man. A natural progression from cheating the tax man is that it is reasonable to cheat all Government institutions – 'after all, we pay for them...'.

It is then only a short step to the view that any large institution is a fair target for a little sharp practice – 'they are so large that they won't really notice...'. Banks and insurance companies are obvious potential targets for this approach and one can see examples every day. Why should it stop there? Can many of us put our hand on our heart and say that we have stood totally aside from this trend? I doubt it. Yet there is clearly a need for each of us to examine our conscience and ask ourselves where such changing standards may lead us. And if, as I have suggested, such slippage has taken place among our 'business leaders', how can we expect the 'man in the street' to refrain from cheating?

Conclusion

Let me conclude by summarising the main points I have been trying to make. The role of management is to set the tone for the company. This involves balancing the interests of various stakeholders. It is here that some conflicts can arise. It is my view that some simple tests, like the 'newspaper test' will normally allow you to see your way through these conflicts, but I would be the first to acknowledge that my experience has been limited. I hope that some of you with greater experience will put me straight if I have over-simplified the situation.

I have also expressed some concern about the consequence of tax pressures on the methods being adopted for the remuneration of executives – issues which are magnified by the salary restraint imposed upon State-owned companies. I see little hope of this situation improving until personal tax rates are lowered.

I must conclude by standing back from the difficult issues I have raised. They do not arise every day or in every company. It is my experience that at least 95% of Irish business is run with integrity. But it is worrying that the public only hears about the remaining 5%. We should try to ensure that the public also hears about the successes and the integrity of the 95%.

A Union Perspective

Peter Cassells

There is a grave danger that the current controversy over business ethics will do enormous damage unless there is an open honest debate on this matter and a code of behaviour for business people put in place. I believe that a proper debate and a code of behaviour would benefit honest business people.

The concern expressed by trade unions about business malpractice should not be seen as anti-enterprise and anti-business people. If we are to create more jobs and survive in the new Europe, we must improve the quality of our entrepreneurs and expand their numbers.

We need an entrepreneurial revolution in this country. We will have to stop thinking of business people as confined to those who were born with a silver spoon in their mouth or those who went from rags to riches by suspect means. Unfortunately in Ireland too many of our business people fall into this category. The public perceive the formula for business success in this country as a combination of pulling strokes, greasing palms, knowing the right people and playing safe at all times. This may not tally with the economic textbooks definition of business acumen, but it is close to what you will be told anywhere more than two citizens are gathered to discuss the affairs of State.

The most corrosive influence on morality in Irish business to-day is the 'Cute Hoor' syndrome, which can be summarised as 'Take as much as you can get and give as little as you can get away with.' This syndrome is made up of business people who are experts in taking everything that the State has to offer – grants, subsidies, facilities for their business, health care for their families, education for their children, free transport for their parents – and who are equally expert in dodging taxes, by-passing regulations and avoiding their responsibilities to the State. They will also take all the goodwill and effort they can get from their workers while paying them as little as possible.

The 'Cute Hoor' syndrome thrives in an environment where it seems to be morally acceptable to cheat the State. Tax inspectors have been criticised from the pulpit for doing their job, but we have yet to have a pastoral on the immorality of tax-dodging.

By 'closing a blind eye' to these offences, the culprits are allowed to feel happy that at worst they are guilty of only minor misdemeanours. Refusing to pay their fair taxes to the State or fair wages to workers are seen as only venial sins. And, since no number of venial sins can add up to a mortal sin, they can carry on happy in the knowledge that they have nothing to worry about – either in this life or the next!

For these business people, enterprise is not about the challenge of making profits by developing new products or providing new services and employing the workers to do the job. For them enterprise is all about buying, selling and hiding – buying cheap, selling dear and hiding the profit.

The 'Cute Hoor' syndrome is not interested in developing an enterprise culture – they are satisfied with making an enterprise out of cunning.

A legally-binding code of behaviour for business people would be the most effective means of ensuring that ethical standards are observed in all business dealings. Such a code would benefit honest business people who believe in fairness and decency, while penalising those who cheat taxpayers and workers. Such a code would have to be legally enforceable. A voluntary code would only be observed by those who need it least and ignored by those for whom it was intended.

ICTU has been seeking more openness in business dealings and easier access to company information for both workers and the general public. Recent disclosures highlight the need to introduce these reforms as a matter of urgency. Regulations governing business operations especially in relation to ownership, acquisitions, mergers and the use of loan notes as a means of reducing liability for capital gains tax, must be made more effective.

The growing use of Jersey and the Isle of Man as 'legal' addresses for Irish owned companies is a cause of serious concern to Congress. Means will have to be found for curtailing the activities of those who, while abiding by the letter of the law, are clearly in breach of its spirit. More and more Irish tax-payers are growing cynical about why so many Irish business people find it more convenient to run their businesses from an address in the Channel Islands than from the country in which they live and where they make their money.

An Environmental Perspective

Emer Colleran

'No generation has a freehold on this earth. All we have is a life tenancy – with a full repairing lease.' The fact that this statement was made in 1988 by the former British Prime Minister, Margaret Thatcher, illustrates the dramatic growth that has taken place over the past decade with respect to public concern for the environment.

This concern has been slow to develop in Ireland by comparison with other member States of the European community. Only about six years ago, an EC survey listed Ireland as having the lowest level of environmental awareness within the community. This, in a sense, was understandable, since public concerns in other EC countries had been triggered by local problems which were not being encountered to the same extent in Ireland – dying forests in Germany, acid lakes in Sweden, gross sewage polluting of the Mediterranean. However, the unprecedented fish-kills of 1987, and the media coverage they received, shocked the Irish public out of its complacent view of Ireland as a green, unspoilt and pristine environment and provoked an awareness that our environment, too, was under threat.

A public reaction to an immediate local concern can, however, be unfocused in terms of the wider global environment and readily lends itself to the NIMBY syndrome (Not

In My Backyard). This, to a certain extent, is happening currently in Ireland with respect to the potential environmental impact of the pharmaceutical/fine chemical industry. Such an exclusive, and at times irrational, focus on one perceived threat leads to the view that the pendulum has swung too far in the environmental direction and that the creation and maintenance of industrial jobs, in particular, is now threatened by an excessive green concern.

It is vitally important, therefore, to address the issue of man's impact on the environment in a balanced and honest way – and it is only by doing so that we can establish whether there is genuine cause for concern and a need to take remedial action at an individual, corporate or state level.

The environment that we have inherited in this generation is not a static entity – it has been alerted and shaped by man's activities over the centuries and over the millenia. The environment is man's primary resource and its use, by man, in every generation, has inevitably wrought significant change. What distinguishes us, however, from our forebears, is the scale of the environmental changes we are effecting in our generation.

A July 1991 document, produced by the EC in the context of the proposed Fifth Environmental Actions Programme, highlights the 'scale, scope and nature of environmental problems today' in the following terms:

'The world is currently on history's steepest growth curve: this century alone, the world's population has increased threefold, economic activity twentyfold, use of fossil fuels thirtyfold and industrial production fiftyfold: about four-fifths of this growth has taken place since 1950. Such growth and its attendant environmental impact constitute an increasingly grave challenge to the very habitability of the Earth.'

This document reinforces the historic European Declaration on the Environment signed by all the heads of State of the European Community at the Dublin Summit Conference of June 1990. The declaration opens with the following paragraph:

'The natural environment which forms the life support system of our planet is gravely at risk. The earth's atmosphere is seriously threatened. The condition of water resources, including the seas and the oceans, is causing concern. Natural resources are being depleted and there is growing loss of genetic diversity. The quality of life – indeed, the continuation of life – can no longer be assured if recent trends remain unchallenged.'

A further quotation serves to highlight the complexity of the global environment problems we face in this generation and the need for urgent and informed remedial action:

'The human population and man's economic activities have grown, since the nineteenth century, to such an extent as to interfere seriously with natural phenomena by complex feed and feedback mechanisms that we do not understand and whose effects we cannot predict. Human society has become an actor capable of influencing our global environment on a planetary scale and may soon have to pay a high price for it, unless we make use of our ever-growing knowledge with longsightedness and with humility.' (Professor Umberto Columbo, Chairman of FNEA, Italy, 1990).

As a biologist, I appreciate the use by Professor Columbo of the word 'humility'. We have forgotten, over the past hundred years, that man is as dependent as any other species that swims or flies or crawls in or on the land and water of this planet. We have forgotten that we are part of an ecosystem that has developed over the millenia and that is totally dependent on the finite resources of the planet on which we live. The conservation of these resources – i.e. their wise or sustainable use – is the rationale for our continued existence.

The massive global changes we are witnessing today result from the profligacy with which we, particularly those of us in the developed countries, have spent our environmental capital. For too long in the northern world, we have followed a policy of growth and development that has squandered the resources of the world and freely exploited them at the expense of the developing countries and of generations yet unborn. We must now rethink our policies and develop new strategies which take into account the finite nature of our environmental resources and which promote their sustainable use. This is the challenge that faces us: how can we use the limited resources of this planet in a way that will equitably support a growing human population and, at the same time, maintain these resources for their continued use by future generations?

If we are to meet this challenge, we must first accept responsibility for the global environmental crisis we find ourselves in and examine the ways in which our present policies have caused it. It would be easy to point the finger at government or at the corporate sector and lay both the blame for this crisis and the responsibility for corrective action at their doorstep. But those of us who live in the developed world must also accept that the economic growth and prosperity we have achieved and the lifestyle that we, as individuals, enjoy is possible only because it is denied to three-quarters of the world's present population and is at the expense of environmental resources that are the common inheritance of present and future global populations. The blame and the responsibility is an individual one, as well as a corporate one, and solutions will depend on individual as well as corporate and governmental action.

Many of our present environmental problems can be traced to three separate but completely inter-linked factors:
  (1) population growth,
  (2) energy consumption and
  (3) waste generation.

The balance between these factors is, however, completely different in different geographical areas of the world.

The present global population is about 5.4 billion. According to recent UN statistics, this number is increasing by 87 million per year, i.e. 65 persons per minute or approximately 3 additional mouths to feed every second. The population is expected to stabilise sometime in the next century at 14 billion, almost three times our present population. By far the greatest proportion of this growth will take place in the Third World countries of the southern hemisphere.

As our population increases so does our need for, and our consumption of, energy. Since 1900, world consumption of primary energy has risen from 600 million tons of oil equivalent to 8.2 billion in 1989. More significantly, consumption of fossil fuels rose from 500 million tons in 1900 to 7.2 billion in 1989. The developed countries of the northern hemisphere account for three-quarters of global energy consumption – yet three-quarters of the world's population live in the Third World. *Per capita* consumption of energy in the Third World is over ten times lower than it is in the industrial countries. This provides a very clear example of the way in which finite global resources are being depleted for the benefit of the few and at the expense of the majority.

Quite apart, however, from the injustice associated with energy consumption, our present usage of fossil fuels is influencing the planet on which we live in ways we are only now beginning to appreciate and to an extent that we cannot yet fully comprehend or predict. One of the most serious of our current global environmental problems is the so-called greenhouse effect or the phenomenon of global warming. Two-thirds of the global warming effect has been linked to the burning of fossil fuels which releases carbon dioxide gas (CO_2) into the atmosphere. The build-up of CO_2 and other greenhouse gases in the atmosphere is causing a gradual increase in global temperature. Since the start of this century, the average global temperature has risen by 0.5 degrees centigrade (0.50C). With present energy usage, experts conservatively estimate that, by the year 2050, it will have risen by 2.50C. This may not appear to be an enormous increase – yet it would be half as much, in 60 years, as the total global temperature increase since the last ice-age, 18,000 years ago. Who can predict the changes in climate, the disruptions of world agriculture, the rise in the level of our seas, that will accompany this temperature increase?

To illustrate just one potential impact of global warming, I want to look at sea-level rise. Scientists conservatively predict a rise in sea-level of about one metre by the year 2050 – and one-third of the world's population lives within forty miles of the sea! Higher temperatures have already caused a significant rise in sea-level the world over. Some countries have been able to raise their dykes and to construct other flood-control facilities to protect them against the rising tides. But in the Third World, where there is no money available for such measures, the rising seas are already creating disastrous situations. Low-lying towns are flooded, important coastal farming regions are silting up and millions of people already have had to flee their houses and villages. When one considers that to bring developing countries' energy usage up to industrialised country levels would require increasing present global energy use by a factor of five, the injustice of the present usage of a finite resource becomes only too apparent.

Global warming is just one of the consequences of the energy consumption patterns of our developed economies. Associated also with fossil fuel burning is the production of acid rain which has sterilised thousands of lakes in Scandinavia, which is destroying the great forests of Europe, reducing the fertility of our soil and eroding the very fabric of our buildings and monuments.

At the other end of the scale, the need for energy in the form of wood and charcoal, by the billions of people who live in the Third World, is causing environmental problems that also are of global significance. Eleven million hectares of rainforest are destroyed annually (an area sixteen times the size of Ireland). Although a considerable proportion of this destruction is to provide hardwood timber for export to the developed world, a significant fraction is driven by the energy needs of the indigenous population. The rainforests are unique ecosystems and are the planet's richest treasure-trove of living things. Three-quarters of all the species that creep or run or swim or fly live in the tropical forests. The variety of plant, insect, and microbial life present is immense. Yet we are destroying this irreplacable pool of genetic diversity before we have even had a chance to properly evaluate and catalogue it – or to determine its potential value to man in terms of potential crop species, sources of medicines and other valuable drugs, chemicals, etc.

The consumer society we have developed in the northern hemisphere not only depletes, in an unbalanced way, the energy and other finite resources of the planet – it also generates more and more waste. We are now only beginning to realise that there is no convenient global rubbish bin – the waste we create stays with us, whether we dispose of it by landfill or tip it into our rivers and seas or discard it to our oceans or, by incineration, transfer it to our atmosphere. Such pollution recognises no national boundaries and puts at risk the air we all breathe, the water we all drink, the soil we all cultivate, even the ozone layer that protects the global population.

These are some of the direct global environmental consequences of our consumer society. There are also, however, some direct local impacts on Third World countries – impacts which we rarely take into account and for which the responsibility is both individual and corporate. A potent example is provided by the fast-food industry. To supply the hamburger market – for example in North America where beef consumption per head of population increased from 38 to 61 kilos per annum from 1960 to 1976 – meat companies began to look for sources of cheap beef in other countries. The rainforests of Central America were considered to offer excellent prospects as pastureland. In Costa Rica, each year, between 50 and 70,000 hectares of forest have been destroyed in recent times, largely for cattle ranching purposes. Ninety-five per cent of meat production is exported to the US while meat consumption within Costa Rica is decreasing. Tribal communities, which practised a sustainable form of agriculture in the forests and surrounding lands, have been driven out and now eke out a meagre existence on other lands that are susceptible to erosion and desertification.

Meat production, even in Europe, has direct effects on the agricultural patterns of developing countries. A large part of the fodder used in European intensive animal husbandry comes from developing countries – soya from Brazil, tapioca from Thailand, etc. For example, soya supplies from Brazil meet 30% of the European Community's demand. Since 1965, the soya-growing area in Brazil has increased twentyfold and now represents 18% of the country's agricultural land base. A recent study has shown that 88% of soya is now grown on land that had formerly been use for labour-intensive crops, such as rice, beans, potatoes, etc. Where previously seven to eight labourers had been employed in growing produce for the local market, now only one is needed to tend the soya that helps to produce the European and American meat and milk surpluses. Meanwhile, food production for local consumption has decreased in Brazil, foreign export income is largely used to service the national debt, there is an increased need to purchase foreign-produced food, and the native farming population is increasingly forced from the land into the shanty-town areas of Sao Paolo, Rio de Janeiro and other cities.

There are many other examples that may be cited as ways in which the consumer society of the north impacts negatively on what was once a sustainable form of agriculture in Third

World countries. The subsidies and other incentives that stimulate food production in North America and Europe, even in the absence of demand, are playing, in a very real way, a major role in the erosion of sustainable, less intensive forms of agriculture in the very areas of the world where food production is most needed.

We must, in the developed world accept responsibility, at all levels of society, for the impact that our lifestyles are having on the billions of the Third World and on the common global resources of air, water, soil, the carbon cycle, etc. We must recognise that there are limits to the type of growth and economic development we have been promoting during this century. And we must ensure that we do not continue to use, in a non-equitable and non-sustainable way, the common finite resources of this planet.

When asked by a British Colonial adviser whether he hoped to raise India's living standards to that of Britain after independence, Mahatma Ghandi replied: 'It took Britain half the resources of this planet to achieve this prosperity. How many planets will a country like India require?'

If we are to establish a sustainable lifestyle on a global basis and in an equitable fashion, the decisions we will have to make in the northern hemisphere will not be easy ones and may well be painful in terms of the resource usage we now enjoy. Clearly, the responsibility for these decisions do not lie solely with governments or with the corporate sector – individually, all of us must play our part in the creation of a new form of society, a society based on positive sustainable policies on a global basis which, in the words of the Brundtland Report, 'will allow us to meet the needs of the present without compromising the ability of future generations to meet their needs.'

Accounting
and Corporate Responsibility

Margaret Downes

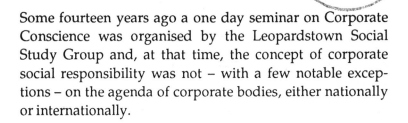

Some fourteen years ago a one day seminar on Corporate Conscience was organised by the Leopardstown Social Study Group and, at that time, the concept of corporate social responsibility was not – with a few notable exceptions – on the agenda of corporate bodies, either nationally or internationally.

In 1962 Milton Freidman, the distinguished US economist, writing on capitalism and freedom, stated that 'few trends could so thoroughly undermine the very foundations of our free society as the acceptance by corporate officials of a social responsibility other than to make as much for stockholders as possible. The business of business is profit.' Freidman's oft quoted view on social responsibility as a 'fundamentally subversive doctrine' was substantially in line with the thinking of most corporate leaders.

I gave a talk at that seminar in January 1978 emphasising that my talk was not authoritative but merely a personal view on complex issues, many of them impossible to define precisely, let alone measure. Can I today repeat that view, stressing complex issues and if not impossible to define let alone measure, most surely difficult to define and difficult to measure.

I also said it was important to put Corporate Social Responsibility into perspective and that the ultimate concern of all organisations and individual managers must be to manage their affairs and the resources at their disposal economically, efficiently and effectively. The problem is to combine sound economic and good management performance with due concern and regard for wider social and ethical considerations. This concept was neatly captured by recent *Sunday Times* billboards and headlines stating 'Balance Between Profits and Principles.' The headlines were referring to published extracts from Anita Roddick's book, *Body and Soul*. The balance between profits and principles is the challenge for corporate leaders.

The corporate responsibility debate was never as lively in Europe as it was in the United States where serious questioning of the traditional role of business emerged in the 1960s. By the early 1970s in the States, social responsibility had become an important part of the landscape, illustrated by:

significant public figures arguing for and against the concept;
widespread debate on the subject;
major companies appointing Vice-Presidents for social responsibility, and
the development of business ethic codes.

The social responsibility debates looked dramatic and appeared to signal a substantive reappraisal of organisational life but, leaving only a small legacy, the energy passed away quite rapidly.

On this side of the Atlantic, concern was expressed about

the need for corporations to be socially responsible but there was little evidence of serious organisational change to address this subject. Organisations did spring up offering and encouraging social audits, and concern for corporate social reporting got as far as green papers and white papers in the UK and, for a brief time, got onto the agenda of the accounting profession. The only real experience in the public domain from this time arose from the work of independent organisations, such as Social Audit Limited and Counter Information Services. These organisations collated information from any source available and produced reports on employee, consumer and community interests, as also on environmental issues. The experiments lasted only a few years and demonstrated how difficult a full social audit of an organisation could be. However, they provided a host of ideas and experiences which have been followed since in various ways.

The past couple of years have seen social responsibility firmly back on the agenda and the public perception of those who express concern at clearly unacceptable industrial practices are no longer mocked as 'anti-progress' or 'unworldly'.

The poor publicity gained by large corporations such as Union Carbide's disaster at its Bhopal plant and Exxon Oil's calamity in Alaska has focussed the mind of corporate management. There is a wider recognition of the hitherto ignored truth that environmental costs will be paid by somebody at some stage, even if the payment is made by a different generation or community or country. Disagreeable demonstrations of this truth include our attitude to 'acid rain', where poor controls of pollution in our factories and power stations are blighting northern European forests and the events at Chernobyl in 1986, where poor management of technical and organisational controls had far reaching and tragic consequences many miles and potentially many years away from the disaster site itself.

Individual nations and businesses overlook the impact of global implications at their peril. In Europe, the EEC had laid the foundations of environmental legislation which must eventually be included in the statutes of all member states. Public awareness of environmental issues has probably never been higher.

On a wider scale, many developing nations are now recognising the damage their own economies and environments face if they remain the West's dumping ground. Given the extent to which companies operate as multinational enterprises, and the increasing consolidation of international communities through the EEC and other treaty organisations, legislation to manage and control environmental issues now appears inevitable.

It is difficult to define where corporate social responsibility begins and ends. Recent traumatic experience in large Irish corporations, on which I do not propose to comment, might be perceived as falling within the corporate social responsibility remit. Recent UK experiences such as the BCCI and Polly Peck debacles and the Homes Assured insolvency certainly fall within corporate responsibility.

An article in the *Daily Telegraph* of August 31st last questions why the prominent politician, Sir Edward Du Cann, who was Chairman of one of the country's biggest companies plus the former Finance Director of British Telecom, Douglas Perryman, were associated with Homes Assured – a tacky little business.

'The most shocking aspect of the affair is not that both men were associated with a company which went bust, but that either of them ever considered it the sort of company to which they should lend their names in the first place. Their presence would remove any doubt about Homes Assured's business, both in what it was doing and how it was doing it.'

One might well ask who is beholden, answerable, for corporate social responsibility at these levels, let alone account for it.

What then is meant by social accounting? A broad definition might be:

'Social accounting involves the publication by a company or other organisation of information to enable parties to assess its performance in social terms rather than just in terms of profitability. Social reports would include information on the corporation's effects on the environment and on the local community, together with information on customer satisfaction and employee welfare.'

Next question: Who will account? Who will measure and report?

Thirty years ago, when the corporate social reporting issue first appeared in academic and professional circles, the arguments against accountants becoming involved in the so-called 'social accounting' matters far outweighed the positive side of the debate. The arguments against becoming involved were based on the belief that accountants dealt only with financial numbers and statutorily required information, that accountants report only to managers and shareholders and that accountants did not have the skills.

Today the argument is not whether accountants should play a role in corporate social reporting but rather how much accountants can contribute to the way in which business is conducted in the 1990s. Environmental issues, business ethics, employee welfare and customer satisfaction are now critical subject matters for the corporate sector and the question is how best the accounting profession can become involved. Professor Rob Gray in his study, *The Greening of Accountancy*, published last year, revisited the ability of the accounting profession to contribute and participate in a social accounting framework. I quote his views:

'A frequent objection to the notion of accountants becoming involved in social accounting was that our skills prepared us for neither attaching financial numbers to social phenomena (workforce data, contribution to communities or environmental impact, for example) nor dealing in the non-financial numbers that might better describe the social phenomena. The irony is that accountants *qua* accountants have little requisite talent in the more traditionally accepted activity of ascribing financial numbers to economic activity. Whilst the experienced management accountant comes to understand the economic processes of his/her organisation, the training as such gives no insight into real issues of (e.g.) chemical manufacturing, mining or the production of new financial instruments. Yet management accounting will claim to cost, appraise, report upon etc., just these activities. This is more obviously the case in financial accounting and auditing where statements of 'true and fair views' will be made about numbers generated from industrial, commercial or service-delivery activities about which the accountant *qua* accountant knows little or nothing. An accountant has no knowledge about, for example, the life of specialist machinery, the state of completion of a chemical plant, shipping law, net realisable value of inventories, or the fair value of a warehouse. And yet the accountant will attest to the numbers which purport to represent them. Furthermore, the profession has been demonstrating for some time that attaching financial numbers to intangible assets, or to anything in times of inflation, is not one of its strongest suits.

It seems probable that we over-rate our talent in this direction and, by implication, under-value the very real talents we do employ. Underlying the systematic collation, sorting and recording of data lies a well-developed conception of information systems. In many regards, the most important talent of the accountant probably lies in the design of, recognition of, assessment of and control of the information systems in an organisation. That perception extends to information systems outside the organisation and, in putting these internal and external systems together, the accountant can generate data, evaluate its probable reliability and determine its appropriateness to the issues under consideration. It is the quality of the systems upon which he/she relies which determines whether or not that value, cost, accrual or provision is likely to be an apposite one. And so, in the same way that the accountant must rely on others for the valuation of inventory and fixed assets, work-in-progress and provisions, etc., so may the accountant equally rely upon others for the measurement of sulphur dioxide emissions, biological oxygen demand or site toxicity. The principles seem identical even though they are not part of current accounting convention.

This ability to design and work information systems would probably not be enough to explain the accountant's position. The accountant also brings (a reputation for) a wider set of abilities relating to independence of mind; intelligence and innate intellectual capacity; experience; evaluative ability – particularly with regard to evidence; broad perspective; a logical and systematic approach; and experience in the communication of information. Such characteristics are hard-won and, one can only hope, are real abilities rather than just matters of reputation.'

The possibility of the reporting function of accountants extending beyond the basic financial statements for investors has been acknowledged – however reluctantly – over the past ten to fifteen years. The information reported to investors has increased substantially (some would say overwhelmingly) and information has been published for groups other than investors. Studies have shown that investors are not completely indifferent to social and environmental information and the introduction of the value added statement and the continuing interest in Employee Reporting have kept the issue alive – even if it still remains marginal in the accounting orthodoxy. In 1989 the Pearce Report, which represents a milestone in Britain's environmental policy, raised many questions about the role of accountants in the new green order of corporate responsibility. The report's most controversial point is perhaps the distinction it makes between two types of capital – namely, man-made and natural capital – and the need to strike a balance between the two to ensure that this generation passes the same value of capital on future generations.

Solutions as to how to strike this delicate balance between man-made capital items like roads and heavy industrial machinery and natural capital like clean air and water are in short supply in the Pearse Report but the report did raise two important questions:

- To what extent has the enormous *per capita* rise in income in the West been at the expense of the capital of future generations, and
- To what extent have the West's economic fortunes been at the expense of both the income and capital of third world countries?

The mere fact that these questions were raised suggests the acceptance of the accountancy profession's role in the environmental movement. These days the consensus is that accounting is more than a form of applied micro-economics. It is a discipline and a profession with very strong political, social, economic and environmental components.

Professor Lee Parker, from the Accounting and Finance Department at Flinders University in Adelaide, Australia, believes, as indeed do many others, that accountants may have placed too much value on their ability to work with figures and not enough emphasis on other key elements of their training, such as information systems evaluation and design, auditing and the collection and evaluation of evidence. He reasoned that 'social accounting can provide figures for things like the cost of installing emission control equipment or the relative effectiveness of various public sector departments, so why shouldn't the profession be able to take this accounting system further?'

Though the spirit may be willing, thus far the profession's body of information experts has not tackled the difficult question of how to balance the cost of man-made and natural capital and, more especially, how best to assign numbers to natural capital items.

This task will have to be faced by management accountants within our larger corporations sooner rather than later. If management is to make sound informed judgements on matters of highly complex social, political, economic and environmental importance, members of our profession must start doing the sums, considering all possible angles and permutations.

In a recent comparative analysis of corporate social disclosure practices among leading companies in the US, the UK and Australia, James Guthrie and Professor Lee Parker found that Australia fell far behind the other two countries. Only 56% of Australian companies disclosed social information in their annual reports as opposed to 98% of UK companies and 85% of American companies.

So far as Ireland is concerned, basic corporate social disclosure practices would have been included in annual financial statements over the past few years – emanating from the Companies (Amendment) Act of 1986. This Act requires that all but small companies disclose information on employment issues such as average number of persons employed, wages and salaries paid, social welfare costs and pension costs. Information is also required on research and development – so long as it is not prejudicial to the interests of the company.

A first comprehensive survey of the published accounts of Irish companies was issued last year. The criteria for including companies in this survey were:-

- Republic of Ireland registered listed companies;
- Northern Ireland registered listed companies;
- UK registered companies with a listing on the Irish Stock Exchange, and
- Large commercial semi-state companies.

The thrust of this 1990 survey of Irish published accounts was to examine contemporary practice in corporate financial reporting in the context of statutory, professional and Stock Exchange requirements. Corporate social reporting was not formally addressed but the survey did establish that, excluding the statutory information just mentioned, of all the 125 companies included in the survey only 5% referred to staff training and development policies, while 9% disclosed their policies of encouraging staff involvement and fostering communications with employees.

Interestingly, the incidence of a voluntary disclosure of social information was highest for semi-state companies and such disclosures were most commonly included in the review of operations. Aer Rianta disclosed the average number of days lost per employee through absenteeism while An Post referred to improvements in its industrial relations record and the productivity agreement with a trade union.

Reference to their social, environmental and cultural contributions to the community was made by 12% of the companies surveyed. These included contribution to the economy by Cadbury Ireland PLC, community related activities by Aer Rianta, regional development by SFADCo, conservation by Bord na Móna, social contributions by the Bank of Ireland, employment creation by NADCORP, and policy on the Irish Language by An Post.

The survey of Irish published accounts 1990 specifically names Cadbury Ireland PLC, Bank of Ireland and NADCORP as being good examples of social reporting on their social, environmental and cultural contributions and, whereas one must give these companies credit for being ahead of the posse, I would have to say that the level of 'voluntary' social reporting by Irish public companies is minimal, is included in Chairmen's and Group Chief Executives' statements and reviews and, as far as I can establish, does not measure, quantify or audit the information. This is not to say that corporate social disclosure practices among leading companies in larger economies than ours is substantially better.

Few would possibly disagree with the view that corporate social disclosure practices and corporate accounting will become an issue in boardrooms in the 1990s. Disclosure, accountability, independence, integrity, good corporate citizenship, energy efficiency, pollution avoidance and cost effective operations are not just the language of corporate leaders but of the ordinary people who are concerned about fundamental issues such as employment, health and the environment. The 'need to know' group is extending daily.

To meet these growing needs, the accountancy profession is being called on to offer more than simple reactive responses to the complex network of issues surrounding the requirements for increased social disclosure practices. There are, unfortunately, no easy solutions and much hard work must be done within the international accounting profession to develop more comprehensive systems involving both qualitative and quantitative techniques which can then be put into practice through the entire business community.

The Role of Taxation in the achievement of Social Justice

Miriam Hederman O Brien

The first requisite of justice, whether social of legal, is that persons in the same situation should receive the same treatment. The tax system must therefore ensure that this element of 'fairness' operates in the State's relationship with its citizens when it collects revenue from them. This might be regarded as self-evident were it not for the other uses to which the tax system is put – as an alternative to policies in areas of economic activity where it is used as an incentive and as a remedy for failings in the social area, where it is used as an alternative to other forms of intervention. The use of the tax system for purposes other than the collection of revenue which is to be used to run the State and to implement the policies which are decided by the legislature in a democracy, inevitably clouds the issue of equity, leads to inefficiency and ultimately defeats the secondary objectives which it has been designed to achieve.

The Taxation of Companies

People tend to think of companies as an alternative source of Government revenue to themselves – indeed, the very phrase 'corporate taxation' conjures up a mental picture of large conglomorates despite the Irish reality of many small and very small companies. Whether large or small, inanimate organisations such as companies do not bear the burden of any tax they pay. Tax collected from them is paid by their shareholders in lower dividends, their customers in higher costs, their suppliers in lower prices or lower volumes of goods and services, their employees in lower wages and salaries and the labour force in fewer jobs.

This transfer of the burden is no reason why companies should pay lower taxes than individuals – or even that they should pay none. It is simply a reality which should be recognised by legislators, policy-makers and commentators.

The existing system of individual and corporate taxation contains many inconsistencies as a result of which business can make very costly mistakes unless major decisions are taken in close consultation with tax advisors. The 'tax avoidance' industry which operates to use the system to the best advantage flourishes because of the flaws of the system and it would be unrealistic to expect business management of any enterprise to ignore it. The individual employee will probably have neither the scope nor the means to make similar arrangements (and indeed will cling to such measures as are available, such as health insurance and mortgage interest relief). Such a divergence creates resentment at the lack of opportunity to 'do as the company does,' irrespective of whether or not the company's tax activities contribute to the well-being of the employees.

Resentment is not a good base on which to run a democratic society. Nor does it contribute to co-operative efforts to improve the economy and create more jobs. It is a stumbling block to the achievement of greater social justice – not because the inanimate corporations cream off profits to themselves but because the impact of the tax system is arbitrary and because tax anomolies divert resources and energy into areas which would not receive priority under criteria of business efficiency or cohesive policy.

In the Irish situation, where there is an urgent need to create sustainable jobs, to compete internationally, to provide the infrastructure for the State and the economy to function effectively and to provide a decent standard of care for those unable to do for themselves, it is imperative to get the correct mix of taxes. From the viewpoints both of justice and efficiency the closer the tax treatment of income from different sources the better. And the sooner that it is acknowledged that 'companies' are legal entities which depend on people to make profits, create business and pay taxes, the better. And financial instit-utions should pay tax on their income in the same way as any other business: on their profits.

Progressive Taxation
A second, and more difficult aspect of 'social' justice is the extent to which the tax system should be progressive, that is, how much more should be contributed proportionately by those who have more and to what extent it should be redistributive, that is how the money gathered should be allocated.

Almost all modern tax systems draw on different kinds of income and activity (or inactivity) to collect revenue. There are direct taxes on incomes, indirect taxes on goods and services, excise duties on alcohol, tobacco and other special products, taxes – either national or local – on property and taxes on companies and individuals. Some countries, such as Ireland, still rely on older levies such as stamp duties, and betting carries a special levy in most Western countries. It is therefore possible to reach a very wrong conclusion about the total impact of the tax system by concentrating on one or even two sources of taxation without reference to the total package.

It is also misleading to draw conclusions about the extent to which the State is reallocating resources by considering the tax system in isolation. A tax system may look as though it is taking a great deal from the wealthy (however defined) but its spending pattern may not in fact redistribute much to the poor – it may be recycling, at considerable expense, much of the funds gathered to those from whom it has taken the high proportion in taxes. As far as the very poor are concerned it is the spending policies of the State which are the most important and the most immediately relevant.

On the other hand, a tax system which includes every kind of income as part of the tax base and operates only personal credits rather than complex allowances would gain more revenue from 'high net-worth' individuals. In the same spirit, if business profits and costs, including inflation, were properly computed for tax purposes, there would be no need for many of the 'incentives' which now distort the system.

There is one category of taxes which arouse particular emotions, both in favour and against, and that is taxes on inheritance. Since most inheritances are built up through the efforts of many people, some of whom have been better rewarded than others, the ability of their owners to leave them, free of tax, to their offspring would seem to perpetuate social and economic inequality. On the other hand, the desire to transmit the fruits of one's labour to the next generation is perceived as acting as a positive incentive to enterprise and the kind of productive effort which is good for the whole economy. My personal criteria are straightforward: once provision has been made for family obligations in accordance with the law, any individual is free to leave his or her personal wealth as he or she wishes. The recipients must then be taxed on the basis of the income to which they have become entitled. This treatment not only satisfies the perceptions of both freedom and justice but also helps to ensure that the resource or asset is used productively (if only to generate the income to pay the tax) and not allowed to lie fallow because of its privileged tax position. The tax therefore should not be 'penal' because the wealth has been inherited or negligible for the same reason. As the general level of prosperity increases in a country, inheritance becomes a more important source of social and economic inequality.

The simplest tax system was the poll tax of ancient times but the attempt by Mrs Thatcher to introduce it as an alternative to a tax on domestic property was a failure, ironically partly due to its complexities. And the complexities were necessary because of the innate unfairness of the tax. It related neither to the value of the property nor to the ability of the person to pay so it became necessary to have exemptions for the poor, waivers for certain categories, refunds for others and the appeal of a single, simple, local levy was lost. Had it enjoyed greater acceptance this would not have been so important but, coming as it did after a series of reductions in the rate of income tax, it was seen as another shift of the tax burden from those with the highest income to those with less. Hence the importance, once again, of looking at the general thrust of any tax system as well as its details. There is, however, no reason why a properly constituted property tax on all residential housing should not be part of a good, fair and efficient tax system. It widens the tax base, helps to reduce the burden of other taxes and improves the effectiveness of the use of the housing stock of the country.

Indirect Taxation

Value Added Tax and excise duties are the two most important forms of indirect taxation in Ireland and both are affected by our membership of the European Community and by the rates in the UK.

It is strongly felt that essential items should be free of tax or, it they have to be taxed, it should be at a very low rate. It is a natural instinct to forego tax on essentials to protect the poor. But it is better to protect the poor without foregoing the revenue from such tax by increasing direct payments to them out of the income generated by the contribution of the better-off. The Danes, alone among the member states of the European Community, have adopted this approach and a single rate of VAT applies to everything from food to books. Free primary education, on the other hand, includes the necessary textbooks and excise duties operate on a somewhat greater number of products than in the other states. The difference between the Danish and German approach however has created serious problems of smuggling and evasion for the Danish economy – which reflects some of our concern at rates operating across the border in Northern Ireland.

The taxation of 'luxuries' is another pitfall in achieving a fair and efficient indirect system. Whose luxuries? As a non-golfer I would nominate golf equipment, for example, but someone else might designate concerts – and then what would happen to the music industry which is supplying a considerable number of jobs in Ireland?

By definition luxuries are a small category of goods and services and taxing them at high rates does not bring in much revenue, imposes higher costs on the State and law-abiding business and leads to evasion. Even if there were to be agreement that fur coats, for example, were really 'luxury' items the revenue gained from taxing them at one hundred per cent would not fund a small school or health clinic. And those who really wanted them would simply buy them in another jurisdiction. There are better ways of taxing the rich.

The changes which are taking place in indirect taxation must be accompanied by a review of the direct payments given to those in need. The policy-makers must have a very clear idea of their social policy criteria – what they want to achieve on our behalf and how effectively the system of social welfare is doing it. And the systems of income tax and social welfare must be aligned far more closely, if not eventually integrated. At that stage we will be able not only to see where and how 'poverty traps' arise but how to overcome them.

The Place of Charities in the Tax System
The corporate sector in Ireland contributes towards the large number of charities which operate in almost every field of activity. They include all kinds of bodies from voluntary groups which have highlighted special health or social problems and initiated ways of solving them, to educational establishments such as universities and professional institutions involved in research, cultural and business activities.

Charities in Ireland do not pay tax on income 'applied to charitable purposes,' provided the income is the subject of a binding trust for charitable purposes only and the income is applied to the purposes in the trust instrument. Such covenants are used both by companies and individuals. There is no legal restriction on the percentage of funds received by the charity which is used on administrative or other expenses nor is there any body charged by the State with monitoring the distribution of funds by charities.

It is sometimes argued that all charitable gifts to approved charities should be allowed as tax deductions on the basis that it would encourage contributions to worthy objectives and reduce social spending by the State. Apart from the difference of such an approach to the contributions of income tax-payers and those who give the equivalent of the 'widow's mite' and are not tax-payers, it must be recognised that such wide preferential treatment would not necessarily improve the lot of the deprived or reduce the State's obligations. It would certainly boost the 'charity industry' but the lack of accountability, transparency and control involved would be most undesireable.

At present the State partially supports many voluntary bodies. There is no reason why this support should not be increased where the State recognises the value of their work within the framework of social, educational or cultural policy. Recognition of the importance of private and corporate donations to charities is made in various ways and the voluntary, statutory and corporate sectors can improve their level of cooperation even further.

Conclusion
Taxation is extremely important in the achievement of social justice in three ways:

1) It must be seen to treat people in similar circumstances in the same way and not penalise them for the manner in which they earn their income. A tax system should be manifestly fair, not only because laws in a democracy ought to be seen to be fair, but also because the state depends on the cooperation of taxpayers to operate the system. Those who evade tax must therefore be pursued and penalised, not only to recover the income due but also to set the record straight for those who keep the law.

2) the 'progressive' and 'regressive' impact of taxation can only be judged in the context of the overall impact of tax and public expenditure. A higher rate of contribution from those who have greater wealth and resources makes social sense, but the operation of an arbitrary, cosmetic or inefficient surtax, whether direct or indirect, will only give rise to anomolies, injustice and a possible decline in exchequer revenue.

3) the manner in which revenue raised by taxation is spent has a major effect on the level of social justice in the community.

The Responsibility of the Media

Douglas Gageby

Speaking only for myself, and just as a preliminary to a lot of preaching about the virtues of Irish journalists, let me say that while people in this state are often accused of hypocrisy about various things -- sex included, of course – it's nothing to their two-faced attitude to newspapers.

The public writes in to the unfortunate newspaper editor about alleged blasphemies and irreverences and insults to the religion of the majority or the minority and so on. And yet. And yet 169,000 of them – of you, I'll say – buy the *News of the World* on Sunday; 86,000 of them, of you, buy the *Sunday People*; 64,000 of them, of you, buy the *Sunday Mirror* ... and so on.

I don't object to anyone buying the newspapers of any country. I'm just drawing attention to what appears to me to be a slight anomaly in our moral attitudes ... and don't tell me that only the lower orders buy these products!

I grow uneasy when people in authority talk of 'a responsible Press,' for they invariably mean:
A respectful Press.
A docile Press.
A 'nice' Press – i.e. nice to them.
A biddable Press.

The Press has one responsibility: to print the news all the time. All the news it can get its hand on. That is its function. Think of it as a public service like, say, the ESB. As the ESB pumps out current to its subscribers, so newspapers pump out news to their readers. Likewise non-stop.

Good news and bad news. Major news and run-of-the-mill news. That's what our activity and responsibility is all about. Acceptable news and news that makes you squirm. News that is in bad taste, some will say. Someone always does. Gruesome stuff. News made by human beings. Also good news in the sense that Erskine Childers used to plead for. Maybe not enough of that, you will say.

Now this is all very solemn stuff. Let me just interject here that we are aware that many people buy their newspapers for quite other reasons than a thirst for pure news. Some mainly for the crossword or the cartoons, others to check the films on television, and, of course, many for sport which is, too, a major element of news for perhaps a majority of men.

The Duty of the Press

Let me now quote what to me is the basic text for all this. It was as given by Delane, editor of *The* (London) *Times* in 1852. As we know, that newspaper did not always live up to such high standards:

'The first duty of the Press is to obtain the earliest and most correct intelligence of the events of the time, and instantly, by disclosing them, to make them the common property of the nation. The Press lives by disclosure: whatever passes into its keeping becomes a part of the knowledge and history of our times; it is daily and for ever appealing to the enlightened force of public opinion – anticipating, if possible, the march of events – standing upon the breach between the present and the future, and extending its survey to the horizon of the world.'

The Duty of the Journalist
Of the duties of the journalist, *The Times* said:

> 'The responsibility he really shares is more nearly akin to that of the economist or the lawyer, whose province is not to frame a system of convenient application to the energies of the day, but to investigate truth and apply it on fixed principles to the affairs of the world.'

And again:

> 'The duty of the journalist is the same as that of the historian – to seek out the truth, above all things, and to present to his readers not such things as state-craft would wish them to know but the truth as near as he can attain it.'

Some of you may think you detect a whiff of Lucifer about this. In the same way, people often ask angrily: 'Who elected you?' Nobody elected us – although John Healy use to say that he was elected every time you put sixty pence or whatever for your newspaper in order to read him. And we don't make election promises.

The Press and Politics
Delane clearly saw the position of the Press, in the political scheme of things, as independent of any official trammels. Lord Derby, shortly to be the Prime Minister, had been

79

affronted by remarks made by *The Times* about Louis Napoleon. 'If the Press aspires to exercise the influence of statesmen, they have a corresponding responsibility to maintain a tone of moderation and respect,' he declared. 'Not so,' said *The Times*. As between the duties of Ministers and of the Press:

> 'The purpose and duties of the two powers are constantly separate, generally independent, sometimes diametrically opposite. The dignity and freedom of the Press are trammelled from the moment it accepts an ancillary position. To perform its duties with entire independence, and consequently with the utmost public advantage, the Press can enter into no close or binding alliances with the statesmen of the day, nor can it surrender its permanent interests to the convenience of the ephemeral power of any government.'

The Press in a way is the permanent opposition. Governments may grow careless, devious, arrogant. The parliamentary opposition may become lax or self-satisfied. Somebody has to keep pricking and poking and kicking and bucking. The Press. We hope.

But although some readers show a certain affection for this or that newspaper, in general, the Press is not loved.

And it is not always tolerant of criticism.

To some extent it is realised now that readers deserve more consideration when they complain. So in recent years members of the National Newspapers of Ireland Organisation, that is the three Dublin groups, *The Cork Examiner* and *The*

Farmers Journal, have each made a new appointment known as the Readers' Representative. All complaints about the newspaper's contents are channelled to this functionary. It is known that in the past some libel actions have arisen simply because a reasonable complaint was ignored or rejected, a complaint that might easily have been met with a little understanding. But the aim is not solely or even primarily to avoid litigation. It is a reasonable service to the people who keep the paper in existence and who deserve to have their views treated seriously and courteously. An example of responsibility, if you like.

Restrictions on the Press
There are considerable restrictions on the writing and publishing of newspapers, primarily the defamation laws.

In theory the aim of the law here is to enable the citizen to protect his or her good name and indeed to restore it where it has been brought into question.

At present what happens is that, perhaps three years after an action is initiated, a court hearing will take place and if the plaintiff is successful, a large sum of money will be awarded. How that helps reputation is questionable. There is a strong element of lottery in it all. The mechanics of such cases are antediluvian. The delay ridiculous.

The National Newspapers of Ireland Organisation commissioned a report of the state of the law on the Press from Professor Kevin Boyle, then of UCG, and Marie McGonagle also from that law faculty. Mrs McGonagle had long made a study of the print media and the law. John Murray, the Attorney General, at the launch of the work, announced that he was turning it over to the Law Reform Commission.

In due course that commission, under the very able Justice

Ronan Keane, produced an elegant, worthy, consultation paper. Later they produced a rather introverted volume on contempt of court, with lingering traces of the mystical, ritual, quasi-sacerdotal air which the law sometimes likes to wrap around itself. Also a third volume which seemed to many to be unnecessary.

On Libel

Journalists are not merely seeking their own satisfaction here. They are as conscious of their own importance as anyone else and have been known to sue for libel and even to sue fellow journalists and editors. This is not a question for journalists only. It affects the whole community. Ludicrous sums have been given in cases here. Lavishness of award, perhaps copied from some whopping monies given in England against tabloid papers. The French have a sense of proportion in these things. Johnny Halliday, a rock singer, sued a French government agency for a million francs. He won his case and was given one franc damages, about eleven pence. I don't know about his costs.

Contempt of Court

Contempt of court is another hurdle for journalists. To take only one aspect of this: can a journalist be compelled to divulge his sources by a judge? Should he be?

An English judge, Lord Salmon, (British Steel Corporation *v* Granada Television) pronounced: 'The freedom of the Press depends on this immunity (to refuse to reveal confidential sources). Were it to disappear so would the sources from which its information is obtained: and the public would be deprived of much of the information to which the public of a free nation is entitled… '

Confidentiality is at the heart of good journalistic practice.

And confidences are often from the highest in the land. How could a journalist reveal from what minister or even what legal eminence his or her information came?

Lord Salmon went on to explain that a journalist should be obliged to reveal his source only in exceptional circumstances, in criminal cases where the security of the state required it.

I have to put it as my personal opinion that security services are often dodgy enough organisations in themselves. I think that while Lord Salmon takes a reasonable attitude for a judge, there are journalists who will believe that the better part is to maintain silence and accept the consequences, jail often. I will go farther and say that I think every journalist should take this position. This is to my mind part of the responsibility of the journalist.

The Press and its readers
It is unwise to underestimate the reader. In England, it is said, it is impossible to do just this in present social conditions and the *Daily Express* of another day was referred to as 'That huge engine for keeping discussion at a low level.'

It is no part of the mission of any newspaper in this country to set out to be offensive about religion or family or other views sincerely held. But we can be touchy. Recently there was a letter in *The Irish Times* complaining that when Dr Philbin died he was referred to in a heading as merely 'Philbin'. Headline writing is done under constraints of space and time and size of type. But yes, the more formal way is better. Yet a short while later, Cardinal De Lubac died and *Figaro*, the French conservative newspaper, had two mentions on page one. The first headed just 'Henri De Lubac,' the second, a short and eulogistic article by one of their senior men, simply 'De Lubac'. I am aware that the letter to *The Irish Times* pointed out how in the same issue Dean Griffin of St Patricks had been given his proper style and title. The positions could have been reversed.

It has been the norm for *The Irish Times* to receive letters accusing it of being anti-catholic. In my time I more than once got a letter from the other side. One I keep under the glass of my desk. It says: 'I hear a Protestant can't get a job on that paper since you became editor.'

Privacy
Privacy? It's a difficult enough question in an age when government and business and much of our public life is coloured by the public relations approach, when the image of the public figure seems as important as his or her achievements, if any.

There are those in public life who strive to present a cosy face to the world and use the services of public relations firms. Quite legitimate. But at what point does the curtain come down? If there are less cosy aspects of that figure's life? Is it intrusion to look at them? Or must we take the cosy public relations side only?

For the average non-public figure, the Press may be intimidating. For every person who would like to be mentioned in a newspaper, there is surely one who simply wants to stay out of print. This must be respected and is, I believe, generally in the Press of this country.

Print and the Electronic Media
I have been all my life in print journalism. It is still the most enduring medium.

TV can bring the great events into our homes. Famine in Africa. The coverage of recent events in Moscow, not only in their vividness, but in their instantaneous presentation should make of this the most informed and educated generation of all. Pictures on screen arouse emotion and move us, but fortunately for the written press, great events always bring a rise in sales. People want to *read* about it. To confirm what was said or done. TV instructs and amuses and provokes us. The written word stands. The newspaper is not going out of date or fashion. Here anyway.

The Power of the Press
The power of the Press? I wonder. Going back into history, Dev. got into power here against the run of the Press. Roosevelt had all the big publishers against him. C.J. Haughey fought his way back into the lists with not many to back him in the Press.

The strength of the Press lies in its public service to the community. Supplying information and related comment and analysis as an aid to digesting the information. Helping the public to look at events in different ways.

Next to plain news, the various columnists and special correspondents do give you something to measure against your own conclusions. Leading articles are likewise, to me, not so much the voice of the newspaper as an instant reaction to events with the aim of giving you some yardstick against which to set your own opinions.

The Media and Censorship

There is the worry that television brings violence and gratuitous sexual realism into the home. There exists a complaints procedure for RTÉ which, I suspect, is not used by the public as much as could be expected. And, whatever can be done about what goes out from Montrose, no control at all can be effected over transmission from farther afield.

Does it all come down to the attitude of parents in the home? To control in the home rather than censorship from outside? I do not think you can say that while television instructs and enlightens on the one hand, it cannot also influence in a malign way. It must.

It is one of the problems of the age for which I have no answer. And I suspect no one else has one that works, except, 'Don't watch television.' Which is not realistic. Our own TV and radio seem to me to be of very high and consistent quality and a worthy service for the State and the country.

On Being a Journalist

Finally and irrelevantly perhaps, journalism is a wonderful career. Worth anyone's life's work. One of the chief attractions is working with other journalists though it is not the only satisfaction. We produce something entirely different every twenty four hours. It's to some extent a relatively unfinished product each time. For a story which we print at 12 midnight will be overtaken at two o'clock a.m. But then we'll be back next night.

It is our responsibility to be there.

Gainsharing – Towards the Future?

Dr J.I.Fitzpatrick

No thinking person can be happy about the way our economic system performs. In the midst of plenty there is grinding poverty. Our lengthy and impressive record of invention and innovation has resulted in a massive flow of wealth but has not succeeded in distributing it equitably. Instead, the rich get richer, the poor poorer – and the distressing aspect of this is that the situation gets worse, not better. The only corrective measure available is taxation, through which Governments endeavour to redress matters by transferring surplus income from the better off to the poorer sections of the community; but such efforts to redress the balance are largely ineffective and, to a degree, counterproductive. Tax measures inhibit production without eliminating poverty.

One of the obvious culprits in this maldistribution scene is interest, a charge levied by the haves on the havenots. In the last two decades interest has become a major cost factor in companies' published accounts. Allied to the rapid inflation we have experienced during that period, it has not only further distorted the pattern of wealth distribution but has turned us into a monetarist society where money has become the sole criterion of success, individual and corporate.

Yet, important though the interest factor has become, it is

not the real cause of our troubles, nor could its manipulation be used to cure the ills of our system. To a degree it is an effect of the weaknesses inherent in our version of capitalism, not their cause. For the *fons et origo* of those weaknesses we must look deeper into the workings of our capitalist system.

On reflection, the business corporation, in the form of the limited liability company, emerges as the symbol and flagship of that system. It was devised by Victorian legislators as the ultimate vehicle for involving private savings in risk enterprises. For more than a hundred years, following on the industrial revolution, these savings had been accumulating rapidly. Demands for liberalising the limited liability concessions, hitherto available only by special act for enterprises of national importance, continued to grow throughout the period. Protagonists argued that only if protected from the common law risk of unlimited liability could private investors be expected to invest in the green grass undertakings that typified a burgeoning economy. Restricting each investor's corporate liability to the amount of his investment was claimed to be the only way to tap the vast savings reservoir for use in the production of wealth.

It must be concluded that the legislation enacted in 1855, liberalising the limited liability privilege, was successful if judged solely from the wealth-production viewpoint. The limited company was soon to become, and to remain to this day, the most important form of business corporation. It is today so much part of our culture that we are inclined to regard it as permanent and inviolable. It has become the centre-piece of a vast financial structure maintained on corporate financial performance, actual and anticipated. The predominance of that structure has given to our version of capitalism the pseudonym of the 'market economy'. It has elevated profit to the status of sole criterion of corporate performance. The concept of wealth has become obscured in the general acceptance of money as the universal standard for judging business achievement. Our system not only confuses money and wealth, it has produced a power structure as the ultimate end of a money-centred economy.

This distortion of genuine capitalism has come about because the legislation that initiated the limited liability company failed to deal with the distribution of the wealth so competently produced. In concentrating on the rights of the capital factor and overlooking those of its essential labour partner, the law set the scene for the confrontation situation that has characterised employer-employee relations ever since. The obvious fact that, in the effective production of wealth, capital and labour are partners, each enjoying rights and accepting responsibilities, was ignored. Instead, in order to attract investment, absolute ownership of the corporation, its assets and their produce, was vested in the shareholders at the same time as their liability for debts was strictly limited. The rights of the labour partner, of employees, were restricted to the terms of their wage contract. They had no legal right to a share of the profit that resulted from the synergistic union of capital and labour.

And therein lay the inhibiting weaknesses of the legal vehicle designed by our legislators. In devising a form of corporation for the production of wealth, without ensuring its equitable distribution, they failed to complete the job. Yet their concept, because of that failure, and because of its unquestionable success and popularity as a producer, today offers the best solution potential – the best way to readjust the balance, and to do it in such a way that production will increase and all parties will benefit. That solution we call 'gainsharing'.

Gainsharing is self-financing profit-sharing. The primary function of corporate profit is to secure the future of the company, its survival and organic growth. To share any of what we might call 'survival profit' would be imprudent, to say the least. In all cases the level of that survival profit is determinable. It relates to the company's development strategy. All of that profit benefits the shareholders, directly by way of a dividend, indirectly by increasing their company's reserves. Its inequity has certainly inhibited production – today the average productivity of manufacturing industry here is less than eighty per cent. So there is a large gap that can be closed. Management can, and should, plan how to do this, but only the workforce can make the plan work, can earn profits surplus to the normal levels at which survival is assured. An undertaking to share that surplus, once it is achieved, with employees, would be the best way to realise it.

That is what is meant by self-financing profit sharing. It will not eliminate the basic weakness of the original legislation but it does constitute an important first step in that direction. As a cost-free addition to employee remuneration it protects the company's competitiveness whilst increasing purchasing power in a non-inflationary way, to the benefit of the national economy.

Our business corporations today are victims of the original legislation. In conforming to custom by seeking profit maxi-

misation on behalf of shareholders, they are following custom. Only if a departure from custom can be seen to benefit
all parties could they be expected to consider such a course.
Gainsharing, as outlined, is the answer. Those who are gen-
uinely concerned about corporate responsibility in today's
world will wish to pursue enquiries.

The Contributors

MICHAEL REIDY is a priest of the Archdiocese of Dublin, working in Adult Education since 1985, and Director of the Dublin Institute of Adult Education.

DOMHNALL McCULLOUGH is a member of the Leopardstown Social Study Group, Chairman of the Clondalkin Group PLC, of James Crean PLC and of the Planned Sharing Research Association.

JOHN SWEENEY SJ is a Jesuit priest with training in economics [M.A.(Econ)]. He has lived in Ballymun since 1980 and is a Founder Director of the Jesuit Centre for Faith and Justice. He writes and comments on social issues as they address the Churches.

MARK HELY-HUTCHINSON has a degree in Chemistry from Oxford University. He joined Guinness, St James' Gate, as a brewer in 1958. He was Managing Director of Guinness Ireland Ltd from 1977-1982 and Chief Executive of the Bank of Ireland from 1983-1990.

PETER CASSELLS is General Secretary of the Irish Congress of Trade Unions, a member of the Central Review Committee, NESC, and a board member of the European Trade Union Conference.

EMER COLLERAN is Associate Professor of Microbiology in UCG and a former Chairperson of An Taisce. She is a member of the Council of State.

MARGARET DOWNES is a Chartered Accountant, former Managing Partner of Coopers and Lybrand and President of the Institute of Chartered Accountants in Ireland. She is a member of the Court of the Bank of Ireland, Chairperson of Gallahers (Dublin) Ltd, Vice-Chairperson of Ardagh PLC, and a former President of the European Federation of Accounting Bodies.

MIRIAM HEDERMAN O'BRIEN is a Barrister-at-Law. She was Chairperson of the Commission on Taxation and is a Director of Allied Irish Banks. She is also Honorary President of the Irish Council for the European Movement.

DOUGLAS GAGEBY is the former Joint Managing Director and Editor of The Irish Times, having begun a lifetime commitment to journalism with The Irish Press.

J. I. FITZPATRICK is a Chartered Accountant and a Barrister-at-Law. He is a former President of the Federation of Irish Industries and is the Executive Director of the Planned Sharing Research Association.